Theory Paper Grade 6   2010   A
Model Answers

G000071409

1   *There are many ways of completing this question. Either of the specimen completions below would receive full marks.*   (15)

EITHER

(a)   *Chords are shown here with roman numerals AND notes on the stave. EITHER of these methods of notation would receive full marks. Other recognized methods of notation will also be considered and marks awarded accordingly.*

Ib   Ia   Va   Vb   Ia   Ib   IVa   Ib   vii°b   Ia   Va   Ia

OR

(b)

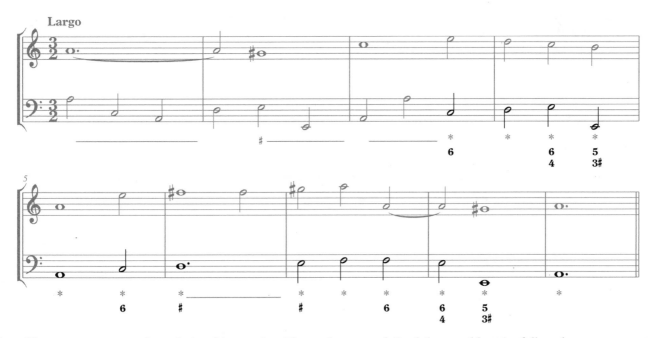

2   *There are many ways of completing this question. The specimen completion below would receive full marks.*   (15)

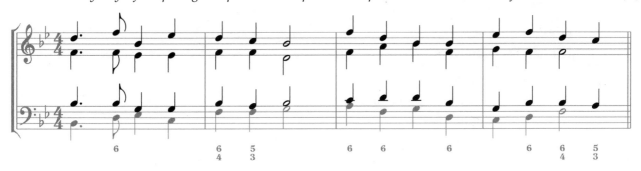

3

3   *There are many ways of completing this question. Either of the specimen completions below would receive full*   (20)
marks. The given openings are printed in grey in order to distinguish them from the completion, but candidates
must include the opening in their answer.

EITHER

(a)   violin

   The source of the opening bars is: Max Reger, Kleine Romanze, Op. 79/e No. 2.

OR

(b)   cello

4   (a)   Chord   V⁷c / V⁷c major   Key   F major   (4)

(b)

(3)

(c)   *All possible answers are shown on the extract reproduced on page 5. For full marks, candidates need to identify*
   only one example of each answer.

   B   Bar   8   (2)
   C   Bar   3 / 15   (2)
   D   Bars   24–27   (2)
   E   Bars   26–27   (2)
   F   Bar   26   (2)

(d)   *One mark will be awarded (up to a maximum of three marks) for each correct reference to the following:*
   left-hand semiquavers / change to minor key / more static harmony / higher tessitura   (3)

(e)   X   diminished 3rd   (2)
   Y   major 9th / compound major 2nd   (2)

(f)   Schubert   (1)

5 (a) with much expression / very expressive (2)

the notes below the sign are played an octave higher than written / play an octave higher (2)

(b) (i)

(3)

(ii) (6)

(c) (i) 6 (2)

(ii) dominant 7th / V⁷ (2)

(iii) 3 / 6 (2)

(d) (i) false $D \Rightarrow G\sharp$ [Aug 4th ?] (2)

(ii) false (2)

(iii) true (2)

Theory Paper Grade 6   2010   B
Model Answers

1 *There are many ways of completing this question. Either of the specimen completions below would receive full marks.* (15)

EITHER

(a) *Chords are shown here with roman numerals AND notes on the stave. EITHER of these methods of notation would receive full marks. Other recognized methods of notation will also be considered and marks awarded accordingly.*

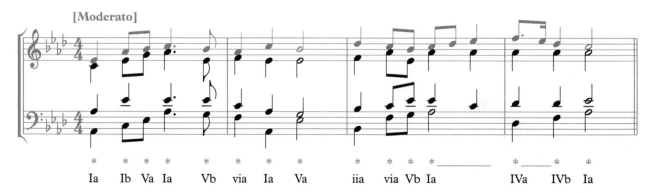

6

OR

(b)

2 *There are many ways of completing this question. The specimen completion below would receive full marks.* (15)

3 *There are many ways of completing this question. Either of the specimen completions below would receive full marks. The given openings are printed in grey in order to distinguish them from the completion, but candidates must include the opening in their answer.* (20)

EITHER

(a) cello

   The source of the opening bars is: Schubert, Impromptu No. 3, D. 935.

OR

(b) oboe

4 (a) always / ever   (2)
          dying away / fading away   (2)
          long / long pause / hold the note for longer than a usual pause   (2)

(b) (i)   perfect 4th / 4th   (2)
     (ii)   F major   (2)
     (iii) 20–21 / 19–21   (2)
     (iv)   7 / 8   (2)

(c) *One mark will be awarded (up to a maximum of two marks) for each correct reference to the following:*
     Similarities   rhythm / ties / melodic shape / slurs   (2)
     One mark will be awarded (up to a maximum of three marks) for each correct reference to the following:
     Differences   dynamics / pitch / notes / pedal markings / octaves in left hand   (3)

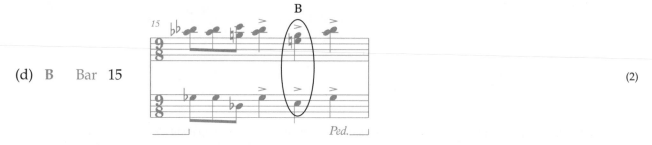

(d) B   Bar 15   (2)

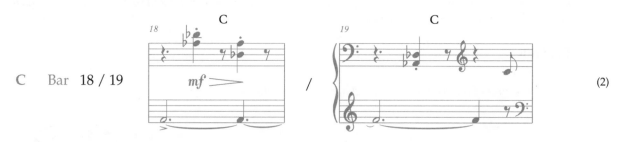

C   Bar 18 / 19   (2)

D   Bar 17   (2)

5   (a)   plucked   (2)

broadening / spreading / getting slower / slowing down   (2)

divided / divided into two parts   (2)

drum roll / rapid reiteration of the same note   (2)

(b)   Clarinets   (6)

Horns

© by Breitkopf & Härtel, Wiesbaden

(c)   1   (2)

(d)   1   perfect 5th   (2)

       2   major 6th   (2)

       3   major 3rd   (2)

(e)   *One mark will be awarded (up to a maximum of three marks) for each correct reference to the following:*

little movement / **pp** / long note values / static harmony /   (3)

     dim. in horns, timpani and strings / reduced orchestration / tranquillo

Theory Paper Grade 6   2010   C
Model Answers

1   *There are many ways of completing this question. Either of the specimen completions below would receive full marks.*   (15)

EITHER

(a)   *Chords are shown here with roman numerals AND notes on the stave. EITHER of these methods of notation would receive full marks. Other recognized methods of notation will also be considered and marks awarded accordingly.*

OR

(b)

2 *There are many ways of completing this question. The specimen completion below would receive full marks.* (15)

3 *There are many ways of completing this question. Either of the specimen completions below would receive full* (20)
marks. The given openings are printed in grey in order to distinguish them from the completion, but candidates
must include the opening in their answer.

EITHER

(a) flute

The source of the opening bars is: Dvořák, 'Silhouette' for piano, Op. 8 No. 6.

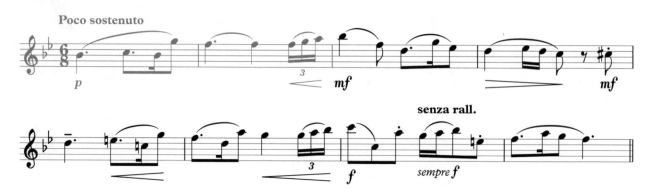

OR

(b) violin

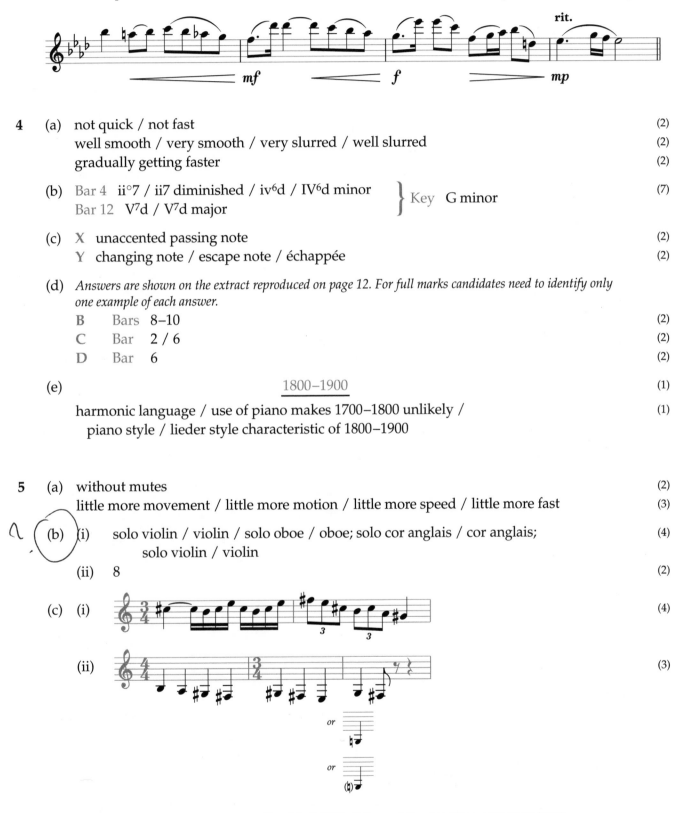

Andante con moto

4 (a) not quick / not fast (2)
        well smooth / very smooth / very slurred / well slurred (2)
        gradually getting faster (2)

   (b) Bar 4 ii°7 / ii7 diminished / iv⁶d / IV⁶d minor } Key G minor (7)
        Bar 12 V⁷d / V⁷d major

   (c) X unaccented passing note (2)
        Y changing note / escape note / échappée (2)

   (d) *Answers are shown on the extract reproduced on page 12. For full marks candidates need to identify only one example of each answer.*
        B   Bars 8–10 (2)
        C   Bar   2 / 6 (2)
        D   Bar   6 (2)

   (e)   1800–1900 (1)

        harmonic language / use of piano makes 1700–1800 unlikely / (1)
        piano style / lieder style characteristic of 1800–1900

5 (a) without mutes (2)
        little more movement / little more motion / little more speed / little more fast (3)

   (b) (i)   solo violin / violin / solo oboe / oboe; solo cor anglais / cor anglais; (4)
              solo violin / violin
        (ii) 8 (2)

   (c) (i) (4)

        (ii) (3)

              or

              or

(d) **1** major 9th / compound major 2nd (2)

    2 minor 6th (2)

    3 perfect 4th (2)

(e) <u>Vaughan Williams</u> (1)

Theory Paper Grade 6   2010   S
Model Answers

1 *There are many ways of completing this question. Either of the specimen completions below would receive full marks.*   (15)

EITHER

(a) *Chords are shown here with roman numerals AND notes on the stave. EITHER of these methods of notation would receive full marks. Other recognized methods of notation will also be considered and marks awarded accordingly.*

OR

(b)

13

2 *There are many ways of completing this question. The specimen completion below would receive full marks.*   (15)

3 *There are many ways of completing this question. Either of the specimen completions below would receive full marks. The given openings are printed in grey in order to distinguish them from the completion, but candidates must include the opening in their answer.*   (20)

EITHER

(a) oboe

> *The source of the opening bars is: Haydn, Trio in C, HWV 27.*

OR

(b) bassoon

4 (a) slow, in a singing style / at ease, in a singing style / leisurely, in a singing style   (2)

(b) Bar 6   V⁷a / V⁷a major   Key B♭ minor   (4)

Bar 21   ii⁷b / II⁷b minor / IV⁶a / IV⁶a major   Key E♭ major   (4)

(c)   (3)

(d) *One mark will be awarded (up to a maximum of four marks) for each correct reference to the following:*
melody is an octave higher / last left-hand quaver in bar 11 / right-hand semiquavers /   (4)
bars 9–11 and 14–15 are four voices / left-hand semiquavers bars 11–13 /
left-hand added quaver in bar 14 / direction of the left-hand crotchets in bars 14–15

(e) *All possible answers are shown below. For full marks, candidates need to identify only one example of each answer.*

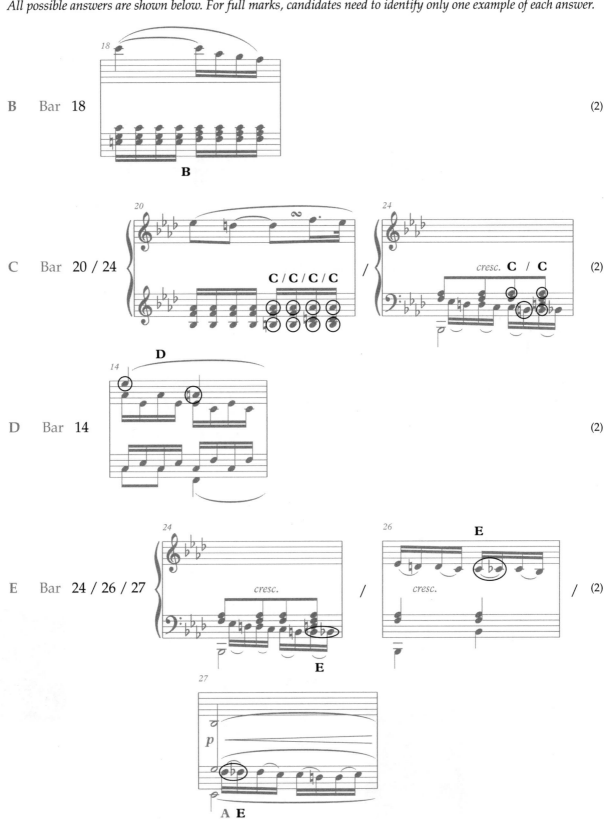

5 (a) with the bow / bowed (2)

sonorous / rich / resonant / rich tone (2)

(b)

(4)

(3)

(c) (i) 3; 5 (4)

(ii) 11 (2)

(iii) 3 (2)

(iv) compound minor 6th / minor 13th (2)

(d) (i) true (2)

(ii) true (2)

Support material for ABRSM Music Theory exams

Theory of Music Exams
Past Papers
Grades 1 to 8 (separately)

Music Theory in Practice
Grades 1 to 8 (separately)

ABRSM
24 Portland Place
London W1B 1LU
United Kingdom

www.abrsm.org

ISBN 978-1-84849-299-8

Published by ABRSM (Publishing) Ltd, a wholly owned subsidiary of ABRSM

Printed in England by Halstan & Co. Ltd, Amersham, Bucks 10/10